God's Promises to a Woman's Heart

Jane L. Fryar

ABOUT THE AUTHOR

A Christian educator for 30 years, Jane L. Fryar currently serves on the editorial staff at CTA in Fenton, MO. She has authored a dozen books and numerous Bible studies, including the popular *Today's Light Bible* devotional material and *Armed and Dangerous: Praying with Boldness*.

Jane holds an honorary doctor of letters degree as well as an earned doctorate in strategic leadership.

In her free time, she enjoys teaching a junior high Sunday school class, baking bread, lifting weights, and playing with Marty the Wonder Dog.

www.CTAinc.com

God's Promises to a Woman's Heart
ISBN 0-9744640-6-6

Unless otherwise indicated, all Scripture quotations are taken from the Holy Bible, King James Version.

Copyright © 2003, 2004 by CTA,
1625 Larkin Williams Rd., Fenton, MO 63026-2404.

PRINTED IN THAILAND

God's Promises to a Woman's Heart

I Will...

$\mathcal{O}$ur Lord speaks these words dozens of times in both the Old and New Testaments. Usually, wonderful promises—almost unimaginable promises—follow.

The poems in this little book grow out of 21 of God's "I will" promises. Think deeply about these promises. Find and read the Scripture passages cross-referenced after each poem. Pray about them.

As you read and meditate, I pray you will hear Jesus' voice speaking his words of concern and compassion directly to your heart!

I pray that, more and more, you will come to see all of Scripture as God's love letter to you in Jesus our Savior.

Above all, I pray that the Holy Spirit will fill your heart and life with joy in our Savior-God's deep love for you!

I will be (*your*) God.
—*Ezekiel 37:27*

Bedrock

When you have nowhere to turn,
Turn to Me.
When you need someone on whom to rely,
Rely on Me.
Please know you can always turn to Me;
you can always rely on Me.

I am the foundation for your future.
No matter what that future holds,
I hold it in My hands;
I hold you in My hands.
(*Hands still nail-scarred by love.*)

Please don't keep Me at arm's length,
Hidden away in the
bottom drawer of your heart.

I want to share My life with you;
I want you to share your life with Me.

✝

Psalm 18:1-3; Jeremiah 29:11-12; Ephesians 3:16-21

I will abundantly bless
— *Psalm 132:*

Benediction

*M*y blessing adds up
to more than a pious wish,
to more than a godly greeting—
much more!

My blessing brings great good,
for when I bless,
I fling wide the windows of heaven
And export to earth some of its essence.

My greatest blessing came to earth
disguised as an infant king,
come to close hell's gates and
destroy death—forever.
An unfathomable blessing,
in a plain paper wrapper.

Now, please believe My personal promise:
I've given you My best,
I won't withhold the rest.

✝

Proverbs 10:22; Malachi 3:10-12; Romans 8:28-32

Chosen

You did not choose Me,
I have chosen you,
and you are Mine forever!

I did not claim you
because of your good deeds, or
because of your potential.

I will not abandon you
when you behave badly, or
fail to live up to that potential.

Nothing you can do
can make Me love you more.
Nothing you can do
can make Me love you less.

I have chosen you,
And you are Mine forever!

✝

Haggai 2:23; John 15:15-16; Ephesians 1:3-8

All that the Father (*gives to*) Me shall come to Me; and (*whoever comes*) to Me I will (*not*) cast out.

— *John 6:37*

Dawning

The sky will disappear
Like a bedroom window shade
snapping up to let
morning's light stream in.
The stars will wink out,
while My angel army
thunders into human history
to gather every son of Adam,
every daughter of Eve.

Then I will open the books,
to reveal the names
of those made clean
in Christ's cross.
Live always in the light of that Day.
Keep looking up for My return.

2 Peter 3:3-13; Revelation 20:7-13; 1 Corinthians 15

I will come again,
and receive you
unto Myself.

— John 14:3

I will cause (*you*) to ride
upon the high places of
the earth!

— *Isaiah 58:14*

Delight

*C*ome! Ride with Me!
Above the hills.
Above the mountains.
Above the clouds.
Through a morning sky of sapphire,
crystalline and pure.

Glide the wings of the wind
As sheer joy lifts your soul
into My presence.

In Me, your life will become
for those around you
an oasis,
a spring of Living Water,
an aquifer that never runs dry.

Delight yourself in Me!

✝

Psalm 37:4; 104:3; Isaiah 58:8-11; John 4:13-14

I will lay ... (*your*) foundations
with sapphires ... and all (*your*)
borders (*with precious*) stones.

— *Isaiah 54:11-12*

Foundations

The pieces of Sarah's
commitments and
carefully coordinated calendar
Went flying across the parlor floor
On the day Abraham came home
to announce a move.
To a tent. In the desert.
On her sixty-fifth birthday.

She never saw that parlor again.
But Sarah saw through faith's eyes
something I want you to see:

Your security does not rest
on houses or salaries or stocks,
But on the bedrock of My love—
My love for you in Jesus.

✝

Genesis 12:1-6; Hebrews 11:8-12; Isaiah 54:11-14

Healing

Here you sit—alone—
In the debris of disobedience,
In the wreckage of relationships
washed up on the shore
of your childishness,
of your stubbornness.

You ignored My Word,
My warnings,
And the abrasions on your soul
provide ample evidence,
produce ample pain.

I will heal your
backslidings.
—*Jeremiah 3:22*

You need not sit here alone.
I am your Savior, your Healer.
I bandage brokenness,
I specialize in
soothing heartache.
By My wounds, yours are healed.

May I sit down here beside you?

Exodus 15:26; Luke 4:18-19; 1 Peter 2:21-25

Homecoming

No matter how hard you try
you can't imagine
the welcome I have planned!

While all the holy angels
Fall on their faces and shout My praises,
I will take your hand
and walk with you down the aisle.
We will stand together
before My Father's throne.

You will wear the sparkling robe of
My righteousness—
the royal wedding dress!
And your heart will burst with joy
beyond any poet's ability
to sing of it.
Your joy will be My joy will be our joy—forever!

✝

Revelation 7:11-12; Hosea 2:16, 19-20;
Revelation 7:14; 1 Peter 1:8; Hebrews 12:2

I will confess (*your*) name
before My Father, and
before His angels.

— *Revelation 3:5*

I will clothe
(*you*) with (*a*) change
of raiment.

—*Zechariah 3:4*

Make Over

From Mud Mania
To Glamour Shots—
That's the change I've worked in you!
Your old clothes no longer fit.
Or should I say,
They are no longer befitting.

The princess you have become
Through faith
In the cross of My Son
Has inherited a new wardrobe,
A heavenly one.
Every new day
My Spirit wraps you afresh
in Jesus' righteousness.

Enjoy the "new you," My beloved!

☩

Zechariah 3:3-5; Titus 3:4-6; Ephesians 4:23-25; Colossians 3:9-11

Open Invitation

My precious daughter,
I keep three things always open:
My door.
My ear.
My heart.
Whenever you come,
(Whenever you come!)
Morning, noon, or night,
I bend low to hear
Your whispered words,
Your scarcely spoken longings.

I yearn to share with you
The secrets of My love, My life, My joy.

My door, My ear, My heart—
These are always open to you.

✝

I will meet with (*you*).

— *Exodus 30:6*

I will send (*the Comforter*) unto you from the Father.

— *John 15:26*

Peace

The Comforter has come!
He has come precisely for
those ordinary days
of your ordinary life:

When every word spoken by a colleague,
—or a spouse—rubs your fur
in the wrong direction.
When every driver on every street
behaves like a 16-year-old
turned loose at Indy.
When one more tiny, jelly-filled fist
or piercing screech
will push you right over the edge.

The Comforter has come!
Let Him remind you of His compassion,
and let Him pour My peace
into your heart.

✝

Joshua 1:5; Deuteronomy 31:6-8;
John 14:25-27; 15:26-27; 16:5-15

I will be with (*you*).

— *Isaiah 43:2*

Real Presence

My daughter, I am with you always—
Not as a disinterested clinician,
dressed in a white lab coat,
armed with a clipboard, and
determined to observe you
like some rat in a maze.

Instead, I am with you
to guard your soul,
to guide your steps,
to give you strength.

No matter how deep the flood,
threatening to swallow you.
No matter how hot the fire,
threatening to smother your life.

I promise I will never leave you,
I'll never leave you alone.

☩

1 Peter 2:21-25; Psalm 48:14; 46:1-11; Isaiah 43:1-13

Rest

I know all about your relentless days,
and your sleepless nights.

I've seen your jangled nerves,
rubbed raw on life.

I've felt the crushing weight
of guilt and sin—
I carried yours all the way to Calvary
on My own shoulders.

And now My invitation stands,
wide-open as My heart:

Come to Me!

Let Me care for your soul.
Let Me lift your burdens.
Fall back into My arms,
trusting Me, trusting My promise.

‡

I will give you rest!
— *Matthew 11:28*

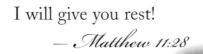

I will love (*you*) freely.

— *Hosea 14:4*

Restoration

You've come back!
Like a little child,
trembling,
and a heart that smarts
with shame.

But you've come!
And that's what matters to Me!

I don't care where you've been sleeping.
I don't care about your
dark alleys and dark deeds.
My love does not come
with strings attached,
with a catch or conditions.

You've come back!
And in the cross of My Son,
I will love you freely!

✝

Psalm 116:1-7; Micah 7:18-19; 1 John 4:9-10

I will reprove (*you*).
— *Psalm 50:21*

Rebuke

When I see you headed for the edge,
hell-bent toward a fall,
My love demands that I warn,
that I rebuke.

But this work is alien to Me;
the language of judgment
is not My native dialect,
For I delight in speaking mercy.

My child, cultivate a tender conscience.
Tune your ears to hear My Word.
Turn at that Word, and live—
live in safety,
live always in the shadow
of My Son's cross.

✝

Hebrews 12:1-6; Isaiah 28:21-22; Micah 7:18-19; Ezekiel 33:11; Isaiah 30:15

Regeneration

Like a rainstorm in the desert
    When the clouds open up
in a bellow of thunder
    And water dances down in torrents ...

So will I pour out My Spirit—
new life cascading into the hearts
    of your children,
    of your grandchildren,
of your students, nieces, nephews,
    neighbors, friends.

Like a desert rainstorm, bringing
    new growth,
    cooling breezes,
    bright hope.

Ask Me!

✝

Isaiah 41:17-20; Joel 2:20-23, 28-32

I will pour My Spirit upon
(*your*) seed, and My blessing
upon (*your*) offspring.

— *Isaiah 44:3*

Shepherd

"The Lord is my Shepherd."
These words count for much more
than any pious rumor.
Let the truth of it
seep into every recess of your soul:

I will feed My flock.

—*Ezekiel 34:15*

I faced the jaws of sin and hell
—for you!
I felt the fangs of death
—to pull you free!
The Shepherd died for every
wandering, foolish sheep.

Now, I will do even more.
I will quench your thirst
with the Water of Life.
I will quell your hunger
with the Bread of Life.
Even in death's dark shadow,
I am and will forever be
your Good Shepherd.

‡

Psalm 23; John 6:35-40; 7:37-39; 10:11-18

Transformation

*M*agicians of yesteryear
boasted of power to turn
straw to gold.
They lied.

But in the chemistry of the cross
I work true transformation.
There, the worthless becomes worthy;
In that cross, I will make
your brass, gold;
your iron, silver;
your stones, iron.

Value.
Beauty.
Strength.

These I create in you
as you contemplate
My work for you.

✝

Romans 12:2; 2 Corinthians 3:18; 4:14-18; Isaiah 60:14-17

For brass I will bring gold.

—*Isaiah 60:17*

Treasure

How deep is your heart?
I will flood it with
My love—in Jesus.

How large are your thoughts?
I will inundate them with
My wisdom—in Jesus.

How wide is your soul?
It will overflow
with true meaning—
in Jesus.

I will fill (*your*) treasuries.
—*Proverbs 8:21*

In Jesus—heaven's Crown Jewel—
You will gain prosperity
Beyond your capacity
To contemplate or contain it.

Colossians 2:1-3; 1 Corinthians 1:30-31; Isaiah 35:1-4; Romans 8:38-39

I will ... honour (*you*)!
—*Psalm 91:15*

Valentine

"*B*e mine!"
You remember the thrill
Of opening the cards—
Long since crumpled and gone,
Like the affection they trumpeted.

But My love for you will never crumple.
Or fade. Or evaporate.
You will be mine on that Day when
I gather My jewels.

The spectacle of sacrifice,
blood-red at Calvary,
Blotted out the sun,
Blotted out your sin.
That sacrifice created
an eternal covenant.

Now let your heart thrill forever
at My promise.

‡

Malachi 3:16-17; Matthew 27:45; Isaiah 44:22-23; Hebrews 13:20-21

Vindication

*O*f all the essential and enriching
things you can learn, My daughter,
This one is key: Learn righteousness!

Not a righteousness arising
from the wreckage of
excuses and self-deceit.
Not an illusion of righteousness,
you conjure up
from smoke and mirrors
and your own imagination.

No, learn the righteousness
that comes as My gift,
that flows from the blood-stained
cross of My Son.

In that cross you are righteous, vindicated, victorious!

‡

Isaiah 26:9-10; Isaiah 54:17; Romans 3:21-25

I bring near My righteousness ...
and I will place salvation
in Zion.

— *Isaiah 46:13*

More "I Will..." Promises from God

Be your God ....Jeremiah 32:38; Hebrews 8:10

Be your shepherd ....Ezekiel 34:23

Be with you ....Deuteronomy 31:23; Matthew 28:20

Bless you ....Numbers 6:27; Hebrews 6:14

Clothe you with salvation ....Psalm 132:16

Come again ....John 14:3

Deliver you ....Psalm 50:15; 91:14-15

Forgive you ....Jeremiah 31:33-34; Hebrews 8:12

Give you a crown of life ....Revelation 2:10

Give you a new heart ....Ezekiel 11:19; 36:26

Guide you ....Psalm 32:8

Hear your prayers........................Isaiah 65:24; Jeremiah 33:3

Help you..Isaiah 41:13-15

Make my covenant with you..................................Isaiah 55:3

Not fail you....................................Joshua 1:5; Hebrews 13:5

Pour out my Spirit...Joel 2:28

Ransom you from death ....Hosea 13:14

Raise you from death ....John 6:44

Seek the lost ....Ezekiel 34:16

Strengthen you ....Isaiah 41:10